I0413349

Mental Branding: M/s Unraveled

A Non-Fiction Manual into the world of Master-Mistress/slave relations and how it all works.

By: Morte

Introduction:

This book is not about kink, it is not about sexual fantasies or how to escape the life you lead because you don't like it.

This is about truth, awareness and acceptance in yourself and how you project it to the world. I am not going to protect you, sugar coat it or give you a romance novel so you can live out fantasies in the bedroom.

I am writing this to empower you with knowledge, self-awareness, self-control and self-esteem. This is where it starts, before the kink, before the service, before ownership, you start at the beginning.

So open your mind to what I have to say, journey with me and learn the truth about slavery and Dominance, learn what is real and what in fact is fantasy.

Walk with me as we explore this fabulous world of M/s and you gain knowledge to live the life you know you should be even if you have not yet admitted it to yourself.

Open the door and step into the world of Mastery and Slavery, I am here waiting.

Chapter One: Who are you?

You have seen the TV shows, the movies, you have read the news, seen the porn, etc.

All those things portray bdsm and M/s in a way that is perverted, blood thirsty, mentally deranged and just plain shameful.

Problem is...they are full of shit. Yes, I said shit. Nothing could be further from the truth than the garbage that is portrayed as *Bdsm* and *M/s*.

That is not how it works, it is not who we are and it is not how we live.

Last I checked we weren't all walking down the street in leather with whips tugging a collared and leashed slave behind us or in some seedy bar filled with smoke, stroking ourselves as we look for our next victim to serial kill.

Is that harsh? Bet your balls it is, I am not here to be Goldilocks, I am here to be real and you should be too, if you're not you will be by the time I get done with you.

So saying that..Who are you? You don't know do you?

I am guessing you're confused, unsure, embarrassed, maybe even mortified that you don't seem to go with the norm of most people.

You stick out, you're different and have strong urges to be pleasing and to make someone happy, regardless if you like it in the moment or not.

It may even be a compulsion for you, a driving need that can't be explained but you don't feel you can stop it; you may have even tried, and found yourself miserable when you cut yourself off from it.

This is called awakening, your mind is opening you up to who you are, it is trying to show you what is best for you, who you are and how to accept it.

Problem is we don't always listen to what our brain tells us, if we did ignorance would not be such a commodity in the world. That is just fact.

So let's take into account you have no earthly idea what to think about slavery in M/s because all you have heard and seen makes you want to run the other way or hide in shame like you are some dirty pervert looking for a way to fuck someone in a dark alley.

The first things you need to know are the qualifications for it. Yes you actually need to have some sort of qualifying standards to actually be a slave.

I am going to break these down in a list and then after I will explain each one in detail and what I mean.

The things you should not have or should not bring into an M/s relationship.

- **Mental illness**
- **Low self-esteem**
- **Dishonesty**
- **Co-dependency**
- **Lack of self-worth**
- **Drama**
- **Selfishness**
- **Me complex**
- **Laziness**
- **Passive/Aggressive Attitude**
- **Assumption**

A big list I know, but then something as important as this is, anything less would be a joke, and people this is no joke. M/s is real and it is the most beautiful experience you will ever find in the form of a relationship.

So let's start..

Mental illness: I imagine that had a few with their backs up, mental illness in itself is not the issue, the issue is when it is untreated or you deny you have a problem and then try to hide in a world where everything is open and expect someone else to fix you.

Doesn't work that way, if you have a mental illness, seek the proper help for it, get the medication you need and then take this journey. Otherwise you will do more damage than good to yourself and that is not the point of M/s.

Low self-esteem: Unlike what is reported by the uninformed about M/s, having low self-esteem is about the worst thing you can do when you're a slave. You project it to others and it does not sit well. Slaves are confident, self-assured individuals, not cowering wrecks of dislike of who they are.

Dishonesty: This should be an obvious one, dishonesty in M/s is like an art thief walking in a crowed gallery and just taking a painting off a wall and trying to walk out with it, it's ludicrous to say the least. In M/s you are laid open, bared soul and all, so dishonest will bite you in the ass rather quickly and cause more harm than good.

Co-dependency: Masters are not babysitters, regardless if they are micro managers or not, you still have to be strong and stand on your own two feet. You can't be relying on someone to *fix* you or hide you from *discomfort*.

Lack of self-worth: I will mention this several times in this book for many reasons but the main one is this. If you have no self-worth then why would someone else see you're worthy? Pride in who you are and what you stand for is a major key to being a slave.

Drama: Bringing bullshit to the table does not mix well when you are a slave or plan to become someone's property. Drama is poison and doesn't belong in the world of M/s.

Selfishness: Forget it, if you are a selfish person you in no way are suited to slavery, you have to think of others above yourself, someone else's pleasure, happiness, etc.

Me Complex: If you have a me, me, me mentality forget about slavery, hell forget about most things. This way of life is not in any way shape or form a world of petty, whiney games of its all about you.

Laziness: This takes work, it is not something you can do from a sofa or laying down, you have to be active or things aren't going to go to well for you in many ways.

Passive/Aggressive Attitude: This just doesn't work for many reasons but the main one being, you aren't in charge and if you play this type of game you are going to find yourself one miserable slave.

Assumptions: Assume nothing, if you think a certain way chances are it is the opposite of what you think, it can also cause grief if you assume a Master wants it one way, when in fact He/She wants it another way. So just get rid of the assumptions and you will save yourself a lot of time and trouble.

This concludes the list of what is not a good idea, it is a broad example but the best over all of what are not really healthy for you as slave.

I imagine about now you are thinking oh hell this isn't easy at all.

You are correct it isn't close to easy, it takes strength, hard work and mental awareness.

But in the end when all is said and done you will relish the journey and love yourself and your life like never before.

Slavery takes a passion rooted deep in the understanding that to be free you first must BE and to be you have to immerse yourself in the entire over all experience of what it is to be a slave.

You know you can, you know you desire it and the urges will not go away.

They will get stronger, you will feel the burning emptiness inside, the need to break free and show the world you're not ashamed to be who you are, who you have always been.

Hold your head high, there is no shame in who you are, there is only beauty, pure clean soul finding happiness.

Life without it is a bleak, bitter landfill and that is no choice at all.

Believe you can be the slave you are, forget the sex, the romance novels, the total lack of substance you have seen M/s portrayed as and embrace the mental branding of true M/s.

The Catharsis alone will change you in ways you can't even begin to understand at this stage.

It can be scary as hell but the more you take the steps into this world the more free you feel.

The more empowered you are.

At this point you still feel the fear, the worry of what will people think! Omg what if society finds out, I will be ruined!

Bah that is such hogwash; let me tell you a little secret about polite society, no matter how snobby and judgmental they are not a one will cast the first stone.

If they did others would question how they even know to speak of it.

But more than that, the more confident a person is, no matter their characteristics people will leave you alone, admire you and in most cases refuse to shun you because you would look Down on them.

I know this will burst your bubble but M/s is in all societies, in all kinds of homes, in all kinds of professions, it isn't just one type of human being, it is tangled into all types, all genders, and all races.

So throw away your fear, it is a waste of your time and energy. Remember no one has the right to judge you for being you.

They don't sleep with you, they don't live inside your head and they certainly are not you.

You got one life to lead, don't lead it in fear of what someone else will think of you. Live it for you not them.

In saying this let us now get down to the heart of it, what it is and how lovely it truly is.

You have discovered so far that this is not some game or insidious criminal act. You know it takes work, understanding and strength.

 Most of all you know it takes a deep understanding of yourself and a lack of fear that you will be judged.

So let me explain to you what slavery is and then we will get to the training of it.

Slavery: It is not about what you can gain it's not some pastime to do on a weekend for fun. Slavery is a deep mental desire to please and serve another human being.

It is the selfless act of seeing only the needs and desires of someone else with no thought to your own. You live and breathe slavery, because slavery is the breath in your body.

It is what you wake up for each day and why you go to bed, so you can serve another day. When you serve a Master/Mistress there is something so freeing, so very fulfilling about it that your whole being shakes with it.

Watching another gain so much pleasure in your servitude is enough at times to bring tears to your eyes

Your total selflessness is a mark to how much worth you know you have, it marks your life like a badge of honor.

It is a mental branding that is not easily found but worth embracing, and relishing

When you kneel and offer up yourself, give yourself so completely, without fear, in total trust in someone else, you break free. It is a heady almost euphoric feeling and you know, just Know that this is what you were made for.

This is the life you are and regardless of what some may say, without slavery you don't live a whole life.

This isn't about sex, kink or romance. This is about mentally giving you over, wrapping your soul and heart around the true essence of slavery.

Will you take the journey?

Will you kneel and give yourself over to the mentality of it?

Can you shed the barriers you placed on yourself and join me as we explore the wonderful world of slavery? Can you live with not trying it? Not understanding who you are for perhaps the first time in your life?

I think not, so walk with me as we explore your world and perhaps dance through it with all the joys it holds for you.

Let me show you a society that is rich in how we live in so far as we are a bunch of people who understands things aren't black and white.

Life isn't always misery nor is it always a dance; it is a mix of the two, because it is real. Not made up, not conjured out of thin air.

It is based on many decades of people and a way of life that is governed by our beliefs in trust, truth and tolerance.

Chapter One: Me

My beliefs are not that of every ones and I take this more seriously than some do, but I am ok with that. If there is anything worth taking seriously with a deep respect and belief in it, it's M/s.

There is no greater joy than knowing you enriched someone's life by guiding them and teaching them to grow into the person they are. Nurturing the soul so it breaths as deeply with M/s as a person can.

I have had the honor of learning and growing in M/s not only as a Dominant but as a slave. My journey as a slave was fraught with some very hellish paths, one of which I almost did not survive from.

This gives me an edge as a Dominant; I understand the journey, the bitterness, the tears, the joys and the triumphant moments. I can look at you and understand what you hide, the barriers you erect so as to move through life untouched by pain.

I know what it is like to break through that, open up and become the exquisite person you are. Your dreams, your passion, your cravings are all there, hidden from the world. This I know.

I know what it is like to lay lonely and weeping as the agony takes hold and you are so alone, wanting so much, yet feeling as if you will never be free, never be able to live as you know you should.

I am here to teach you how to live, how to break out and be who you are, a slave. Take my hand, let me show you my world, let me guide and shield you on your path, I am here. Listen and learn from me and I will show you a world so rich in color you are stunned with it.

I am Dominant, this is who I am but I am also slave, it too is who I am. No I am not what is referred to as a Switch, I do not believe in the terminology for many reasons.

I am all dominant and I am all slave, the two do not mix, the two do not merge and I don't turn one off to use the other.

It doesn't work like that for me. I am both 100%, I know who gets what from me and I accept all sides of me. There is no confusion inside me, it is stark, it is real and it lives.

Chapter Two: Understanding

You will learn many things; most of all you will learn who you are and how to live with your choices even when the world around you can't because of nearsighted bigotry.

I have heard many say your trainer is your owner, I disagree with this for many reasons. The main one is simple, if you are new to the lifestyle and don't know much if anything, it can be a confusing place, some will say research it, some will say watch and learn.

Both are ok choices but when I think of what is out there about M/s I cringe, the material is so far off in so many ways, not all of it but a good bit of it is.

To seek an owner to teach you to me is ass backwards. How do you know that person is even right for you?

How do you know in 6 months you will still want to be with that person?

It can all be so misleading and as you grow and learn you are not the person who started out.

A Master/Mistress is human too and to allow a newbie fresh out of the gate into our world is setting both the new one and the experienced one up for some disappointments.

This is why I stress Trainers; yes every Dominant has their own way of training and wants things done their way.

But let's get real, basics are basics and the teaching of them should be done by a Trainer, it eliminates those who decide this type of way is not for them, and weeds out all the bul shit too.

Those left are true to learning and growing and a Trainer will know who is who.

Dominants become jaded by all the bullshit out there, the frauds, the fakes, the ones looking for a fairytale.

A Trainer weeds all those people out so the true ones can be seen, heard and perhaps owned.

It also protects a new person from stumbling onto someone who is not a Master or Mistress but who is a Predator.

We have a duty to protect those who seek out learning about what M/s is, to shrug it off and throw them to the wolves is dishonorable and M/s is an honorable way of being.

I am speaking from experience, when I started I did not know a thing, I was very young and as a result of this I ended up in the hands of a very sick man.

It can and does happen, that is reality.

Slavery is a beautiful thing that can be made ugly in the wrong hands and it can damage someone in a way that is very mentally acidic.

This is not the type of person I want someone wanting to learn a beautiful thing to fall prey to. Even the experienced can become involved with such an individual.

The mind is a fabulous place to control but in the wrong hands it can become your greatest enemy.

I caution anyone who wants to get into M/s to understand there are dangers, they are very real and they can hurt you.

There is a great beauty and an absolute sense of freedom in slavery that you won't find anywhere else but here in the world of M/s.

M/s is about respect, understanding, learning, growing, guiding and following. It is about give and take, an unselfish need to please another and a clarity of will and strength that you won't find elsewhere.

It is also harsh, self-serving, and lonely at times and it will test your resolve, your conviction and your strength. It is not all rainbows and sunshine, reality rarely is.

I don't want to give the false impression that M/s is a party or walk in the park. It isn't, like anything you care deeply about, there are good and the bad part of it, there is so much beauty, honor and depth.

For such a worthwhile life you have to be willing to make sacrifices, you have to understand that in order to gain freedom and total happiness you also have to give up things.

You're in the box thinking, your sight of black and white, your worry that someone won't like you and your own lack of belief in yourself.

Complete trust in another human being isn't easy by any stretch of the imagination, it can be downright daunting.

To trust in someone so completely is like nothing you will ever experience; there is no hidden thought, worries or shame.

Your open, purified inside your mind and soul because you know regardless of how you are there is a person who knows you inside and out.

It is the one who takes you for who you are and helps you develop that into something even greater.

Sometimes it is hard for someone who doesn't know to understand what I am saying. So think of it like this, remember when you told your best friend your inner most secret and they still were your best friend.

That feeling of relief and happiness was grand, well take that and times it by 100 and that is what full disclosure to another feels like.

No barriers, no hiding, pure open trust and acceptance. That is what it is about.

Learning to be who you are is also learning to give of yourself completely if you choose such a path then there is little you can't do, little you can't accomplish in your life.

In saying this, you can't just say hey I am a slave or I am a Master/Mistress, it doesn't work like that, it takes time to develop and grow, through learning and understanding.

Putting a title on yourself doesn't make it so which seems to escape a lot of people out there. I could say I am the Queen of Sheba, that doesn't make it so.

Titles are only good when they are deserved or given; otherwise all you are doing is playing at it. The whole well my way is not someone else's when it comes to M/s makes me want to slap the dog shit out of some people.

Everyone doing things differently doesn't mean the foundation and symmetry change. It has been around a lot longer than most of you have been born, in some areas of it, no one on earth was alive when it started.

So trying to say that isn't how it goes is like saying men have babies not women. I know, amusing isn't it?

I think one of the biggest myths out there is that Dominance is achieved by how you dress, the whip you hold and how well you bark out orders.

To me all this signifies is you like leather, are a bully and can only accomplish the control of someone by using a weapon. One of the biggest areas that are widely neglected in Dominants is manners.

You don't have to use brute force or vulgar language to control and lead. If you own a slave and they are mentally branded by you or if you are just starting out owning someone, a please and thank you does not qualify as weakness.

When giving an order saying please does not mean it is a choice, and if you have the control no slave is going to think you are asking them to do anything but it is a sign that you see them as more than just a robot.

Thank you works the same way, it doesn't cost you a damn thing in your dominance to say thank you when they complete a task or when they say yes M.

Politeness is an indication of not only self-control but a sign of totally being comfortable with yourself knowing you control your world and those in it.

Same goes for emotion, I am a whiz at taking emotion, putting it in folders inside myself and using them only when I think it is appropriate.

However, as a Dominant showing emotion is not a weakness either, in most cases the showing of it leads to a stronger bond between M and s.

If you show you care then the more they will strive to please you. Without emotion a slave will burn out fast, they will lose the desire, drive and love of slavery.

In a sense you ruin the very person you took it upon yourself to protect and nurture. That to me is not an acceptable action from a Dominant; it speaks of misuse, sloppiness and lack of leadership.

Most seem to forget dominance doesn't mean you have to act like a prick, it should be natural not forced and it should never be about the need to make someone suffer because you don't feel good inside.

A true leader can lead with a look or gesture; they have no need to use props or force. They are, there for people follow regardless.

I am sure some are having a hard time with this concept and they find themselves frustrated at the lack of obedience in the person whom serves them, if it is a constant battle then chances are the person who are with is not a slave. It is that simple.

The only time this is not the case is if you have a damaged slave, one who has been through hell and back and fights who and what they are.

That can be daunting and frustrating on many levels. Denying who we are is damaging in so many ways, this type of situation is when de-conditioning comes in.

If faced with that type of situation you will have your work cut out for you. I will speak of it more later in the manual but I want to get back to you as a dominant.

Now we all know slaves have no choices, no options they do as they are told and that's that. I agree as a slave but I do not practice that type of dominance to its fullest.

Learning human nature means you learn just what people are like, their quirks, how they function, who they are.

In doing so I have come to realize no matter how great a slave someone is, you can kill it in them by being to Masterful.

Yes there is such a thing. I believe even as a slave someone should have choices, now before you yell bullshit let me explain this concept.

I tend to give someone two choices, sometimes three depending on the circumstance, I know generous of me!

These choices are usually when something is hard for a slave, oh sure I could say tough do it anyway and brush aside their inner turmoil and conflict.

I tend to be of minds that if it is hard give them choices so the original order doesn't seem so bad.

Even if they feel it is not really a choice it still gives them a sense that you care enough to give them a choice in the first place.

This can strengthen the bond between you and often makes them strive to be even more obedient. I don't advise giving choices for every little thing, but things that are hardest for them.

Empowering a slave is a good thing. Acting like you are stiff with constipation all the time doesn't make you more dominant, in most cases you just look like an ass.

If you can't trust in your slave enough to give them the freedom of empowerment and self-worth then I have to question your motives and your purpose.

This may seem harsh but a Dominant is confident in who they are and doesn't need to control by fear or force, it should come natural and be in the very make-up of your being.

It should never feel forced or as if you are acting out a part.

That goes the same for a slave, it should come natural to you even if awkward at first, it should never be forced or just a moment of fun for you.

It should come from the deepest reaches of your soul and should slowly beat like a heart, slowly growing stronger as you grow.

Chapter Three: The Master/Mistress

Before I begin I want to say this real quick: I will use the term Mastery for both Mistress and Master, because regardless of what sex you are, you have to have Mastery in what you do.

I am not big on the whole title thing personally, I go by Mistress Morte for this manual and those to follow because a very dear slave male I call friend gave me the title and in honor of him I use it.

He is an amazing person and if he chooses such a term for then I am proud to wear it.

I have also been called Mistress Death by one sweet little female slave whom I also call friend. So in saying let's begin…

Just like with slaves, there are things you should not carry with you into M/s and I will list them as I did about slaves.

Here is the list, learn from it.

- **Unreasonable Anger**
- **Abusive Disposition**
- **Low Self-Esteem**
- **Lack of Self-Control**
- **Expectations**
- **Assumptions**
- **Obsessive Possessiveness**
- **Total Disregard for Humanity**
- **Lack of Respect**
- **God Complex**

So let me explain these, some I am sure you know but to be clear I will still list them.

Unreasonable Anger: If you cannot control your anger, if you tend to get angry for no reason or your anger sweeps in at the littlest of things, then you need to work on that before you try mastering anyone.

Abusive Disposition: This one should be a given, it is one thing to be a Sadist and a whole other thing to be an abusive asshole. The two are not even close to the same thing. If you like to abuse people then you need to leave M/s in shame, this life is about honor, respect and dignity.

Abuse has no room in it and only a coward uses abuse to control another.

Low Self-Esteem: There is nothing worse than a Dominant who claims they are one and then whines.

If you do not have the self-esteem to think you are a great catch, an actual slave is going to laugh at you when you come whining how you can't find a slave.

Here is a wakeup call, chances are they run when they see you coming because no Master/Mistress would whine or chase after a slave.

So work on you before you make a fuck twat of yourself, embarrass yourself and give M/s more bad rep. It has enough idiots running around doing that without you adding to it.

Lack of Self-Control: This should be obvious, if you can't control your own actions, thoughts and emotions then you sure as hell have no business trying to control someone else's. Basic logic, to control you have to Have control of yourself.

Expectations: If you walk into this thinking you're going to be the next by-blow with a harem, think again.

Expectations will find you becoming resentful and worst case scenario you wind up in a corner somewhere rocking back and forth mumbling "

Omg it's not real, there are no naked slaves running around to be picked up like litter on the side of the road, sniffle, sniffle. "

Assumptions: This one is a good one, assuming is becoming lazy in your mastery over another. Just because you give them a list of what is expected, it is still YOUR job to inspect the work at the end of the day.

Don't assume it got done because you decreed it; this will end with a slave slowly slacking off, simply because the structure they know goes to hell, because you were too arrogant in your Mastery to keep them feeling secure in that said mastery.

Obsessive Possessiveness: Jealousy is an ugly, ugly little demon and one that can destroy you. No I am not saying share with all and be merry.

However, just because your slave tries a new perfume/cologne before going to do morning errands doesn't mean she or he is banging the bag boy at the local market or that he is meeting a new lady to fuck in her car. Trust is the key, remember.

Total Disregard for Humanity: If you think everyone is beneath you or you have no regard for a person in need or in trouble who sincerely needs help.

If you scoff at someone who got robbed or shot, if you find you could care less about people in general without a kind word for anyone then you need to find your soul my friend because without it Mastery isn't achieved.

Human decency and kindness teaches us many things.

No, I don't mean be all sunshine and roses, going around singing "You are my sunshine ". I mean show respect for the people who share the same space with you who are decent human beings and not the dredges of the earth.

Lack of Respect: Even slaves deserve your respect. They aren't your slave because they *have* to be, they are your slave because they want to be.

They see in you're the Master/Mistress they have been seeking, so respect it. If you don't then you aren't cut out for M/s. Respect has a lot to do with M/s and it is a mutual respect, not one sided.

God Complex: I know this is a hard one for some, but you aren't God and Goddesses, you are flesh and blood, you make mistakes, you show emotion, you are not an all divine being who is perfection.

Sorry to burst that little bubble, but we my friends are human. I know it is a sad, sad realization but hey at least you still have coffee, bacon and cheese right?

This concludes the list of things that shouldn't be going on inside you, there are many more as I stated in the slave section but these cover the basics.

My form of Mastery is not this new age stuff, the main reason is simple, what has worked for years and years shouldn't be tweaked, changed or messed with.

This is not an in the box thought process. It is simple logic, don't fix what isn't broken. Unfortunately along the way someone thought "Damn this shit is too hard, hey I'm going to start my own way and call it M/s and shout, "We are all different and live the life differently".

Whoever did that, I hope someone shoved a foot up your ass because you have made a mockery of M/s and a bunch of people followed behind you because they are too lazy to actually work at something worth working at.

Harsh again I know but I have sat and slowly watched M/s be eroded into this circus for freaks, a beautiful, deep way of life turned into a mockery is a travesty.

I don't need a title, I don't need 50 slaves behind me to verify I am Dominant, I don't need to put on a corset, boots and swing a whip so people think I'm a Mistress.

You are what you are regardless of some fad or kink you have going on.

You don't need props to make you a Master/Mistress, all you need is yourself awareness that you are who you are and a slave, they are kind of essential in the scheme of things.

But they don't make you who you are; you make you who you are. If you want your slave to call you Master, Mistress, Ma'am, Sir, Honey Bunches of Sweetness or Fucker go for it.

Just don't walk around like a name makes you something, a name is empty without the actions, thoughts and projections of a well-controlled, knowledgeable, commanding presence.

It's as simple as that or not so simple. Depends how you look at   it.

If you are always right, chances are you will be one lonely right person, it takes true strength and honor to admit when you are wrong.

I hate to burst another bubble, but you aren't right 24/7, you're just not that perfect, none of us are no matter how much we wish we were.

Admitting you are wrong is not a weakness, it isn't some taboo action that will result in the death of a 1,000 virgins. Be wrong, own it, learn from it and move on.

Strength of character is something everyone should have. Nor do I believe a person is just one set of characteristics, one type of person.

Versatility is a key to Mastery, processing a situation in the blink of an eye, figuring the variables out.

Being ready for any given situation gives you a bigger sense of not only your own surroundings and control but also a broader scope of the world around you.

I'm not talking paranoia here, I don't mean arm yourself with a gun and look out your window every five minutes then in a fit of hysteria shoot the neighborhood cat that ran across your lawn and you mistook it for a zombie.

I mean learn to adapt to a situation that you may or may not have foreseen, keep your mind open to all possibilities and all situations.

This will further help you develop a keener outlook and thought process which is very valuable in M/s and in life in general.

Not to mention how much it enriches your soul and mind. It's called Brain food. The more you expand your mind the hungrier it will be and the more you will take it, understand and learn to control it.

Mastery is not for the lazy or the weak nor is it for the conceited abusive ass. We abhor true abuse in M/s, it is below our beliefs, not part of an acceptable practice and we help those we see being abused.

What we do isn't abuse, it isn't some crime on humanity or a human being. What we do is consensual; we get consent and give consent.

We don't just steal someone off the street, throw them in a cage and beat them until they fall in love with us and would rather cut their legs off than leave.

That isn't M/s that is a sickness that sadly is around the world in many places. Consent is huge in our world, you may only give it once, but you damn well know what you are doing, why, how, and for how long by the time you do consent.

This is not some cloak and dagger situation. You are fully aware of what you are doing as a slave and as a Master or Mistress you have taken the time to explain, demonstrate and clarified exactly what they are consenting to.

We don't hide behind this life; we aren't bullies, murderers or insecure mentally ill people. We are Doctors, Lawyers, Writers, Policeman, Politicians, Teachers, Judges, etc.

We are everyday people who simply opened our minds and eyes to the way of things and in doing so; we evolved and became the people we were meant to be.

For some it lays dormant for others it is there and we seek out the feelings with a sense of unabashed curiosity. There is no shame in the people we are.

The only shame is in the judgments people place on a way of life they have no clue about and don't bother to truly find out the heart of it.

This is my world, this is where I thrive and no it isn't some cookie cutter life but there is so much honor, integrity, self-awareness and deep commitment in it. Even now many years from the beginning of where I started it can make me pause with the beauty of it.

Chapter Four: Reflection

The biggest thing people seem to forget or ignore is the fact the self-reflection throughout your life is needed, especially if you are in M/s.

Along the way people lose that drive they had, yes I am sure people had a part in causing you to lose it, but whether slave or Master/Mistress, you and only you has the ability to control how you feel about yourself.

If you dwell on it then you are only harming yourself and maybe even those around you. What you project has a major impact on your life. This life doesn't give a lot of room for self-failure when it happens over and over because you refuse to get your shit together.

Same goes for shame, if you feel shame at being a slave or Master/Mistress then you have it all wrong.

No we aren't like everyone else but there is a hell of a lot of us out there and too many seem to think we are a group of 50 and so you hide, feel shame, feel fear.

We damage our way of life in some ways more than the vanilla world does. Many scoff at that but it is true. The view we give the world is so guarded.

So wrapped up in the sexual kink and perversions that it is no wonder the vanilla world continues to act like we are spawns of Satan.

Our image is important and it has been tarnished not just by vanillas but by our own kind.

Due to our lax attitudes we have let a bunch of people turn the lifestyle into a circus show of pure carnality. We don't fight for the truth, for the complete essence of M/s.

We complain about it amongst ourselves or tell one of them off, but the whole compliance thing has turned what is a beautiful thing into the local bazaar for every type of freak and idiot out there.

People speak of how it was yet do nothing to change how it is. Accountability in all things my friends, it starts with speaking up.

I am perhaps old school and some call it a dying way of life, that pisses me off.

The only reason it is not embraced now more so then in the past is people have become lazy mentally and physically. You want to learn what this is about, then listen and learn.

Don't try to go off and make up some *new age* M/s. Where it is all about sex, leather and how loud you roar.

I will be the first person anywhere to say how much I love sex, kink, torture, etc.

But I can't live on the total lack of depth revolving around the notion that sex and kink is M/s.

There is passion, seduction, a desire like no other when you live the mentality of it.

Your soul is fed completely right along with your mind, and that people is worth diving into and licking it up like salt on your hand before tequila shots.

Some may not understand this and that is ok, it takes time to delve into the inner workings of this life. It is not an overnight catharsis and you have a journey ahead of you.

A lot of eternal thought processing to go through, sort and understand. It can be overwhelming but it isn't impossible, if it were no one would be doing it.

There are some really good people who are in the life of M/s. Learn you, reflect on those things which you are puzzled at and seek out the mental framework of it all.

Learn where it is coming from inside you. Hone the skills and walk the path. You will be much better off when you do so.

Onward we go from here…

Chapter Five: The Male Slave

This is a subject I will be very careful in describing, representing and informing on. Not because I don't know a thing about it because I do but there is a male slave named

Ellis aka keds55 who has touched me deeply in so many ways as a friend and if anyone could stand up and be the poster man for male slavery it is this man.

So this part is because of him and for him. May I give it the honor it deserves.

This branch of M/s is one of the two choices that have been made the most mockery of, it is so tainted and marred by bullshit that most judge it before they even take the time to delve into it and learn about it.

Whether you are a male slave or not learning another way of life just broadens your own knowledge of the way of things.

Unfortunately this life choice is by far one of the most sneered at and made fun of, of choices.

Why? It is because of the idiots running around out there claiming to be a male slave. In my own experiences I have come in contact with more fuck twats and misinformed males then I can count.

I'm talking everywhere, online and off line. It is about enough to make you want to scream at the injustice of it all.

But I am here to change how you think and how you act when it comes to male slavery. There are a few big no- no's when it comes to your thought process and you need to get rid of it because it erodes and mars the sheer masculine beauty of it all.

So as I am known for my lists so you get a list also. Let's begin and delve into it.

- **Whiney**
- **Groveling**
- **Weak**
- **Sex hungry**
- **Size of your dick**
- **Poor you**
- **Belittling**
- **Fear**
- **Loathing**
- **Insecurity**

Let me run these down for you so as like with the rest of lists I do, you have a clear understanding of what I am talking about.

Whiney: Oh this one by far amuses and disgusts me. As a Mistress or Master the last thing we want to see is some man whining that he can't find anyone or how he always fails or people are mean to them.

Christ on a Crucifix, you are a man not a toddler. Put on your man panties and buck up. We don't want to see someone who is always whining about poor them.

You need to start owning who you are and get over this need to self-abase yourself.

Groveling: Ok let me set the record straight on this one, if we want you to grovel we will tell you to. Groveling like that of a "snot faced little kid" just makes you look pathetic.

It frankly is a turn off mentally which means it is a turn off period. Try to have some self-respect, manners and regard for the person you are and the person you are trying to serve.

Weak: Hate to rain on your parade but being a male submissive doesn't mean you are weak. Projecting such a thing just turns us away from you. If you have no value in yourself, we will have no value in you.

Sex Hungry: Sex is a wonderful thing, but if all you are looking for is kinks then chances are no one serious in the life will take you seriously and will not want to own you. M/s is about mentality not porn.

Size of your cock: I don't care what size you are, and this constant need to act like because you have a small cock you are a piece of shit gets old. The cock doesn't make you who you are; you make you who you are.

Poor You: Get over it already, we all have our bad history, terrible relationships and have been shitted on a few times in our lives.

The past shouldn't own you, it should be there to smile about or shake your head at but not to drag you down and make you some whimpering moron who feels sorry for themselves and refuses to let go and live in the now and not the past.

Belittling: The need to let people know what a piece of shit, beneath their foot person you are and how you will do whatever it is that is asked of you regardless if they told you to stab yourself when they don't even own you is just dumbfuckery. Use common sense!

Fear: Fear is a big one as I have stated. Stop being afraid you will be judged just because you are a male slave. People are judging you because of how you portray the male slave.

This is not a very good image. So knock it off, it is unfounded in most cases and just ruins a good thing by tarnishing the strength and charisma of it.

Loathing: If you hate yourself for being a slave or just in general then you need to wake the fuck up. You need to learn to love yourself and become a whole person so you can make the quality of your M/s experience a very good, healthy one.

Insecurity: We all have had them, but if you allow your insecurities to rule you and affect how your life goes then you are in no way living any kind of life let alone this one.

Be proud, stand tall and embrace this life with zeal and passion.

This concludes the list..

Now onto the male slave and who he is. When I think of this I always think of Ellis. I cannot think of a better example out there of a male slave.

Somewhere along the way people got this idea that the male slave was to be looked at with contempt, loathing and pity.

Where you got such a view is beyond me other than the media and such which should have been your first clue that it wasn't how you should live.

To be a male slave takes so much inner strength I admire such men. Yes men, this stigma that to be a man means you have to hold the reigns is such bull shit.

You can be a man whether you lead or whether you follow, which you choose does not dictate if you are a man or not. How you do either does however help define you as a man.

To act like you are beneath anyone is a crime against this life and a crime against the very essence of who you are.

Now let me explain what I mean here before anyone gets their backs up by the whole * beneath* thing.

No human is beneath another human, we are equal in our right to choose who we are and what we become. This is what helps to give you the strength to submit, to let go and become the property of another.

If you are truly beneath anyone then there is no value to you, no worth. There is nothing that defines you, shapes you and makes it possible for you to grasp the intricacies and the mental stamina it takes to be who you are.

To act like you are the scourge of the earth is to deny who you are.

A male slave is something to be proud of, to carry you with dignity and honor. To understand truth and respect is by far a great part of your way of life.

You choose to be a slave; you choose to give yourself over to the command of another. This is the life you choose, because you do so you should feel no shame in which you are.

You should never shrink from people and cower like a beaten dog.

You ought to serve with the very being of you, radiating confidence, honor, dignity, truth and respect. Your job is to be selfless, serving and pleasing.

Tell me how you can do that if you act all poor me and ashamed of who you are. You are a reflection of your owner, what you do impact's your owner.

How you act and live impacts your owner and is a direct reflection of an owners ability to take care of and control their property.

It is a reflection on their character and their competence as a Master/Mistress. So how anyone would think a whiney, sniveling little boy who acts like he is the dredge of the earth is a good reflection on themselves and their owners is beyond my comprehension.

Pick your balls back up and learn that to be a slave is to be strong, intelligent, self-assured and takes work, perseverance and commitment at every angle.

If a dominant tells you different then they need to go back to the beginning and relearn the shit they missed. Leading comes with heavy responsibilities and consequence for the decisions we make.

Every action we take, every moment we lead has two major outcomes, the wrong path and the right one.

It is never easy to lead another who trusts in you so completely, who gave themselves over to be protected by you.

The male slave has it harder than a female in the simple fact men are taught to be the stronger of the sexes.

It is projected as a weakness for them to be anything less than that. So their choice to be as they are takes courage far more vast that most can even begin to grasp.

As a male slave you have a duty to show this life what it is about, the pride you have in it and to teach others the right way of it.

To come out of the shadows and hold your head up knowing you chose this life, you chose to be selfless, strong and obedient.

Whether you are new to the life or old to it, you should have this understanding of who you are and what you are.

If you do not, start over, gain this knowledge and forge your path in our world without shame or fear marring your path.

This is real; this isn't a moment in time, it is a lifelong commitment and choice to be who you are and to lessen it in any way is to make a mockery of yourself and the life.

Learning, training, gaining knowledge, structure and discipline is needed. You have got to train.

You cannot suddenly be a slave, and you don't just wake up one day with the full knowledge of it and go hey I'm a slave today!

Anyone who says they know it all or they don't need a lesson or lessons is full of shit.

I don't care how much training, knowledge and lessons you have had. You will never be such an expert that further training is not needed.

There is not a person alive who can tell me they know it all, I don't care who you are. You're not perfect therefor you continue to need to feed your brain with knowledge and learning.

To fill your mind with a God Complex is not only lazy but it takes conceit to a whole new level. As a slave neither one of those things should be in your make-up. That is a plain hard core fact.

Due to this, structure is so very important in every aspect of your life, in and outside of yourself.

Structure builds an alert mind, character, a sense of balance and an order to the otherwise chaotic existence of life.

The one thing that can ruin a slave faster than anything is a lack of structure and consistency. I have seen it over and over, and you can't just rely on your owner for this in 100% manor.

You have to learn the ability to build structure in your own personal life, yes your owner owns all of you, controls all you do.

However, structure is something you have to maintain as much as your owner needs to maintain it for you.

Even when it comes to micromanagement you still have to do what you are told, self-structure goes a long way in helping you understand such things.

Lists often help you to learn structure, discipline and attentiveness, the more you write it down the more you can train your mind to what you put on paper.

Memorize it, learn it and live it. Write your goals, your rules, what you plan for the day, what you want to see happen in the day and how you will work at succeeding in your thought processes for that day.

Seems complex but it isn't. Writing things down is actually one of the best tools to use when honing your mind to not forget things.

Not to mention it helps build your thought process and reflexes more than you would think at this point. I know this from personal experience which should be obvious.

You need to focus on the mental aspects, forget the sex, forget the kink at this point. You need to learn to serve.

Not domestically, not sexually but mentally. Your job is to bring a certain mind set to the table, to be there mentally for the one you serve.

You need to learn to think of them first and foremost and forget any selfish little idea you have that it is about you. It's not; it is about giving someone joy, pleasure and comfort.

It is about letting them know your loyalty, commitment and acceptance that you will stand for and with them even if shit hits the fan. You're not there to argue with them, to be petty or jealous.

You're there because it is who you are and who they are. You do what they ask whether you like it or not because they want it and it is pleasing them.

It can be tough, harsh and a pain in the ass sometimes, but in the end it enriches your life in more ways than anything ever has.

It is because you know what the vanilla world doesn't, you know what it is to open yourself totally and be free.

You have a duty to yourself, your owner and this life to represent it all in the right fashion. If you don't you need to check yourself at the door and walk away.

Don't bring disgrace to yourself, your owner or this life. It is time to stand and show the world how we truly live.

If you can't do that because you are too whiney or ashamed of whom you are then step away because the life has been damaged enough and it needs to stop.

Learn how to act and how to live; when you can do this you will be whole and happy. Until you do this, you will always struggle and find yourself shunned for the ridiculous way you act.

This concludes the Chapter on male slavery; I have only touched on the basic obvious issues. I will get more in depth later in another manual.

Thank you Ellis for being the man and slave you are, for enriching my life and the lives of others with your kindness, your wit, your intelligence, your strength and your inner beauty.

May we have many more years of laughter, love and wild times to see together.

Chapter Six: The Female Slave

Ahhh ladies, I imagine whether new to the life or an old hand at it you find yourself looking around at people and going huh?

What the fuck? We have all been there, all seen enough to know some people are so far out there they are waving at you from space.

Then there are the ones you just look at and go I need to swallow more for the good of mankind. You may not say what you are thinking but nonetheless you are thinking it.

I tend to say what I am thinking which can have some amusing affects and some oh shit moments.

One of the draw backs perhaps of M/s as a slave I have become so comfortable with who I am that I really do not care what another thinks of me, outside of my owner.

Oh I am not saying I'm rude, spitting on the sidewalk or yelling for the waiter when I go out to eat. I do have manners; however I do not lose sleep or wonder if what I say will make someone not like me.

I am too old, have been through too much and discovered life is too damn short for me to worry about such things I have better things to do with my time and so should you.

I know, society and all, but to be honest ladies if you aren't at a place you feel comfy being you at, chances are you're in the wrong place.

Now let's get down to why you are reading this, slavery. Today's society is so fuckered up with how men and women are viewed it makes me want to slap a few million people.

Yeah I know generous of me, only a few million!?

Somewhere along the line women seemed to forget that even while obeying and serving another you still are all women. You do not lose that just because you choose to obey another.

It ought to make you become more so, be better at who and what you do and help you grow into a more self-assured you.

So like with the rest you get a list too, no need to applaud, I know, I know I'm so giving! Yes, I am grinning here.

I can be a sarcastic shit but by now you should have sensed that about me, if not lay down the crack pipe and pay attention!

Here we go....

- **The Princess Complex**
- **The Attention Whore**
- **The Whiney Bitch**

- **The Limit Hound**
- **The Cra-Cra Hoochie**
- **The Invalid**
- **The Collar Jumper**
- **The No Brat**
- **The Skank**

I know harsh right? But all true so let me get on to defining these. If need be grab a tissue and cry it out when you realize you are one or more of these.

It is ok, there is hope and redemption for you. I am dead serious.

The Princess Complex: Honey unless you actually hold a title and are an honest to god princess, put the tiara down because you look like a dumb ass. This kind of complex as a slave is just stupid, your owner is not going to kiss your ass and allow you to throw fits and act like you are above them or anyone else.

I don't care how good you look; the only men who will kiss your ass are the kind who will pay you for it in some form or fashion. This is totally unacceptable as a slave.

The Attention Whore: Oh this one is the one I find the most amusing by far I think. You're a slave; you're not on a stage on Broadway.

Getting all huffy or upset when someone doesn't pay attention to you or doesn't drop what they are doing to stroke your total lack of self-esteem is so damn silly I can't even believe you would go this route.

People laugh at this type of attitude and in general you are disliked by many for it, especially when you run around claiming to be a slave on top of it. You make a mockery of slavery, of your owner and of yourself. So you need to step back and seriously work on your inner self cause honey you have issues.

The Whiney Bitch: I am just shaking my head over you. Life is so bad, your owner is so bad, people are so bad, whine, whine, whine. Everyone is sooooo mean to you, ok I get it.

Your life is awful, you aren't handed everything right when you want it, and you have to do things you don't like, well suck it up buttercup if you want to be an actual slave it isn't about you. It's about pleasing another and doing selfless work.

The Limit Hound: I will be the first to say limits are to be respected and upheld by an owner. Even as a slave there are some limits that just should be present to you.

However, limits are not like a grocery list, your list should not be full of wont and cant dos. Limits are those things you find beyond reproach, or illegal or completely disgusting. Putting cleaning or taking trash out as a limit is preposterous.

The Cra-Cra Hoochie: Look I understand there are mental illnesses out there, I get that. But acting like you just escaped the nut house or being so out of control you look like a possessed demon from Hades is not acceptable in any form.

Screaming or slashing someone's tires because they don't like you doesn't say much for you as a person and sure as hell doesn't make you any kind of slave. So get some help before you attempt the real world and M/s.

The Invalid: Ok look I understand illness, physical issues and health issues but when you make a martyr of yourself and list 20 different diseases you got going on when half of them should have killed you by now you are giving a bad rap to those who are really hurting or sick.

Seriously if you list three types of cancer, 18 surgeries, 5 dislocations and your big toe was blown off, you need therapy for your head..just go quietly into the night my friend, shhh silently please.

The Collar Jumper: I know it might look cool to be a sci-fi character but jumping from collar to collar like you are teleporting your cunt all over the place is a bit much. Collars have meaning, they aren't toilet paper to wipe your ass on and discard at will.

This isn't a porn movie where you get to pop on and off a Dominant tasting them like they are 101 flavors at the local Baskin Robbins.

Being collared is a beautiful, deep thing and to make light of it is reprehensible and you are no kind of slave that is real.

The No Brat: Calling yourself a brat just so you can run around yelling no I won't all the time is not cool. Brats don't actually act like that; you are trying to top from the bottom and ought to be shoved in a closet somewhere with a binky until you can act appropriately.

There is a time and place for most things but this type of behavior is simply you trying to get what you want and being selfish.

The Skank: For the skinny skank put down the crack bong, grab a cheeseburger and go take a shower and for the fat skank brush off the chip crumbs, remove the stained t-shirt and go take a shower.

No matter where you come from you should dress decent and for the love of god take a shower and brush your hair on a regular basis. Stop being a walking advertisement for a Yo Mama joke. Have pride in yourself!

Ok now that we have gone through that list, I am sure you are somewhat shocked at my harshness. This is ok I don't mind your views, but know this, I am in no way sympathetic to any bitching you may be doing.

I am willing to throw it out there and talk about it; you should be willing to face such things in yourself and change. Slavery is optional in one way, the beginning before you submit yourself to slavery.

After that your word is your bond, you can't just change your mind because something difficult arises. You knew going into it that it's no joke, if you didn't I lay blame at your feet and your owners feet.

Before you give yourself to another in slavery it should be made very clear what you are in for, if it is not then the owner is at fault.

But if you knew without a doubt then it is for you to come to terms with and accept what is in you. You need to step up and honor what you pledged to do no matter how hard it is at times.

Learn to listen, learn your owner, be able to know what they want before they ask for it. Learn to be pleasing on the eyes and on the mind.

Study like you would if in school. Find out what makes your owner tick, what subjects they like, what they don't like. Be prepared to do what it takes at any given moment to please.

Most owners like an intelligent mind, so learn, read, research a number of topics. Be versatile in how you are and how your mind works.

Don't rely on one type of way; make sure that if you are asked something you know them well enough you can answer in an informed, intelligent manner.

Any fears, self-doubt or questions you have, go to your owner, ask to speak of them in a calm, rational, respectful manner.

Communication is always important and you should never hesitate to express yourself as long as you do it in a respectful way with dignity.

This goes for if you are just starting out new with someone or if you have been a slave awhile. It works the same regardless. You can't be a bystander in this life, you have to grab on and go for the ride.

One of the hardest parts for so many see to be the tasks given. The thing about tasks is, once done there done. So moaning over them doesn't do much good.

Getting them done is rewarding internally, especially when you see how pleased you owner is.

Target one task at a time and attack it with zeal and before you know it you're done with them all.

Another thing is organization, get organized, the more you are the easier things will be for you.

You will know where everything is, you will know where it goes and it will give you a sense of accomplishment.

Life is as simple and as hard as you make it and it goes the same for slavery. You can make it as easy or as hard on yourself as you choose to.

What you choose is your choice but in the long run the choices we make affect us years down the road and affect those around us. So be careful how you choose because it will impact you.

I wish you luck in your journey and hope you can come to love and embrace slavery as much as I do. If you do, trust me there is no greater place to be.

Chapter Seven: Discipline

This one is so varied in so many ways. There are hundreds of ways to do this and there are numerous opinions on the subject.

I could write for days and still not finish, but I am not willing to do that so I will just pull some of them out of my brain and discuss them. There I go again being generous!

Here is my list...

- **Assignments**
- **Physical Infliction**
- **Corporal Punishment**
- **Ignoring**
- **Seclusion**
- **Sexual Denial**
- **Ball Gagging**
- **Bathroom Denial**
- **Lectures**

Assignments: I think this is a very good type of punishment, especially if they are writing assignments. It expands the mind and teaches self-discipline not to mention focus which can go a long way in correcting an issue.

Physical Infliction: This is one of my favorites to use personally. Nothing says punishment like physical work. Exercise is a wonderful thing and even if you are an exercise buff this one is still good for you. No I don't mean have them do normal exercise. I am talking boot camp style, 5am exercise.

It differs from normal so they won't have an aversion to regular exercise and it gives them a lot to think on. Whether it is running four miles or biking ten miles. This is a great punishment to get a point across and not too many repeat an offense to get this one again.

Corporal Punishment: To be honest I am on the fence with this one. I see the benefits and the draw backs. Whipping someone for an infraction can have good results they learn from and in some cases if the crime fits it, then by all means whack a mole.

But I also think punishing someone in this way for every little infraction doesn't do much but wear you out and breaks them down, especially mentally. So I think unless it is a major offense this is not the type to use.

Ignoring: Unless you are so furious you can't see straight you choose not to speak in the moment and instead need to get yourself under control I am not sure ignoring is the best thing to do.

Communication is something I stress very much and ignoring your property when they fuck up is in a lot of ways leaving them in confusion and making them think things that are not real relevant to what is going on. But that is just me.

Seclusion: This one I agree with. It is basically the same as corner time. Sit by yourself and think about what you did for a while then we will sit and discuss it.

Have two benefits, one they know you're still there and two they have to think on what they did that was displeasing. It soaks in more for them and for a lot of infractions this one is a good one.

Sexual Denial: This one for punishment is just stupid, you can cause a lot of self-esteem issues and make someone feel totally rejected. No one should be made to feel that way.

I don't care if it is punishment. Some things just go too far and this is one of them. This reminds me of a vanilla woman withholding sex from her husband because she wants something. It is cheap and petty.

Ball Gagging: I wholeheartedly approve of this one. When it comes to back talking or rude behavior to be this is perfect. There is nothing like making them silent when they want to act in an inappropriate manner.

It still makes it to where you can lecture the hell out of them and they can't say a word. It fits many infractions in my opinion and isn't mentally damaging.

Bathroom Denial: Ok making someone hold their bodily functions can actually damage their body and make them become incontinent which I don't know about you but I would rather them have full control of their bodily functions at all times as a slave.

People need to research some things medically before they go doing them. Knowledge is you friend.

Lectures: I love this one, having someone sit in a chair in the middle of the room and look at you while you chew them out really gets the point across and every so often make them repeat what you said so you know they are listening is wonderful.

A ruler in this instance is acceptable; if they haven't been listening wrap their knuckles with it. Soon enough they will get the picture and learn quick.

Now this is my experience and beliefs. I am sure many would disagree but we can't all be as right as I am. Yes, I am grinning here.

Each situation has consequences and is unique. You can't use the same style for everything nor can you use brute force every time someone does something wrong.

You have to find the right balance of tough and strict. Remember you are in charge of your property and their mind is yours. You have to treat it well even when you treat it harshly.

If you constantly drain them you will use them up and then they are not good for anybody. Take care with your property, the longer you take care of it the longer it will be around.

Burn out can happen quickly if you are not careful and discipline is a fast way to have that happen especially when the discipline is always harsh on the mind and body.

Discipline needs to be handled with a clear mind, an understanding that you are doling out punishment to another person regardless that they are your property they are still flesh and blood.

It never should be inflicted spur of the moment, like with anything you control, you need to control what you inflict it, how you inflict it and what the consequences of your own actions can cause.

This is as important a part of this life as is anything else and should be treated with the same respect and honor you give the rest of the life.

It isn't always easy being focused and I control and we all make mistakes. In order to build character mistakes are necessary even if we wish they we not. I don't expect anyone to be perfect, it is not possible.

However using your best judgment as much as you can helps these mistakes to happen infrequently. This goes a long way when it comes to inner peace as well as outer peace.

Accountability is there for a reason and when you make a mistake in discipline, be honorable enough to step up and own your mistake. Move on and grow from it, which is all we can do.

Chapter Eight: Authenticity

There are two quotes I like that I think say much and I want to share at the beginning as we continue on.

I know of nothing more valuable, when it comes to the all-important virtue of authenticity, than simply being who you are.

Charles R. Swindoll

I find more of an authenticity in people who are a little strange - so I really like characters who are just the tiniest bit weird. I find enormous comfort in that - someone who's kind of normal just doesn't feel as true.

Missi Pyle

I think both of these say it all.

Moving on…

I find it so frustrating at times when people seem to think that the life we have chosen is us living in a fairy tale or not living in the real world.

Frankly if this is some fantasy realm I hope I never leave it. I have found more grace, integrity, honor, honesty and commitment in my chosen way of life than I have found anywhere.

Like with any life choice we have our village idiots but on the whole the people are worth knowing.

Just to sit down and have a serious discussion about our views is an opportunity to expand your mind and come to an understanding that is perhaps beyond the reach of a typical mind.

By typical I mean the mind that lives, breaths and sleeps society standards, the invisible standards that are built on bigotry, false actions and the wealth of what you have not who you are.

We are about as authentic as it gets and I say that with pure conviction. The fact that society has dubbed some of what we do, illegal that alone should give you a clue that we are on to something.

Best way to control something is to make a law against it. Problem is instead of studying this life choice and figuring out right from wrong, assumptions are made.

Then there comes fear, offense and downright hostility for a life the general public knows nothing about.

If one were to use logic, wouldn't it stand to reason if we were all these horrors we are portrayed to be, we would all have been locked up and had the key thrown away? I think yes.

So what if we like to be smacked around or smack someone? So what if we tie someone up or are tied up? So what if we give control of ourselves over to another or control another?

Do you live in my house? Can you know for sure I am being abused?

Just because you think something doesn't mean it is so. Live in my shoes or anyone's shoes in the life for a month and then tell me what you see as actual abuse.

We are an authentic way of life, we abhor actual abuse and we stand up and protect those in such a situation.

Can you say the same for the neighbor whose husband beats the shit out of her?

Or the kid who goes to school and you know they are being abused?

No, you choose not to open your eyes to it, because you don't want to see truth. So you tell me which life choice is living in the fairytale and which is living in the real world?

If you can't walk down the street and truly look at what is in front of you, if you can't understand what is going on around you then I suggest you start becoming aware and take the blinders off.

We are real. Are you?

My mother once told me, if you can't be real then who you are going to be because everyone else is taken.

This has carried with me over the years and holds much truth. To not be who we are is to be nobody and I don't know about you but I prefer to be someone as opposed to no one.

Regardless of the *stigma* that comes with being me, it is worth the ride.

Because in the end I can look you right in the eye and say I am authentic, the people I know are and the life I lead is, as well.

I think I will leave this chapter right here, no more needs to be said on it.

Chapter Nine: Things Not Forgotten

I have not mentioned a few types of life choice in detail. I might do so later on in other manuals.

For now I want to give a brief summary of some of them because they have just as much importance as the rest.

Little's: This type of life is probably one of the most misunderstood and disliked of all the life choices.

People automatically assume a little is some sick perversion for a younger adult and an older one.

This is far from the truth. It is actually a state of mind; it is not even a sexual thing. Some people revert to a point in time in their life when they were young, for whatever reason. It doesn't make it anymore wrong or sick than any life choice.

Those who have little's understand it is about a parenting thing, a nurturing way of life. It is not dirty, it is not wrong; it just is how some people are.

Cuckolds: This one I have to say I admire, whether you're a female cuck or a male cuck, hands down to you.

To be able to give yourself over to this type of life takes an inner strength I have not seen in many.

To be so emerged into giving another pleasure as you watch or don't watch while you are in chastity is phenomenal and should never be brushed aside as stupid or that they lack self-esteem.

Cucks have some high self-esteem and are very attuned to who they are and accept it fully and with great passion. It is an intricate way of life and a very, very mental one.

Fetishist: I mention this because regardless of what you do, knowing what you like and not being afraid to embrace it with color and charisma is awesome.

You are not the typical nor are you alone in your likes. They can vary drastically and have many levels. Each one having its own richness and zest, hats off to the Fetishist.

Baby Girls: This is not a little; it is not remotely the same thing other than it is about nurturing and protecting. Baby girls are the playful type female.

They like to play, laugh and be silly. This being said, they are not rude, disrespectful little shits. That is not a baby girl. They also love to be cuddled, protected and have their fears soothed.

But don't mistake them for dummies or weak, you would be wrong. They too have amazing core strength and are intelligent, quick witted females.

If you are a baby girl you have a bounce in your step and a wide passion for living and pleasing.

Dominant for Hire: Now this one I have to say I am not fond of not so much because of what is involved but on of how it is carried out. I don't care what your chosen profession is.

But if you are going to make it a profession and get paid for it, treat it like a business and make sure you represent the business in a manner befitting an actually profession, with dignity and grace.

If you look and act like a whore, people will call you whore. But if you look and act like a professional, you will be treated like one.

So if you want to get paid to do a non-sexual scene with someone more power to you, if you make it what it is and not some seedy, shady looking deal.

Leatheriest: Now the leather community is based on the gay sexual orientation but can be found in other cultures of bdsm.

I have no problem with this and frankly I think in some areas it has some very good points, especially when it comes to protocol and behavior.

They have been around since the 1940's I believe it is, so they have a very nice track record. Whether you are gay, straight, bi-sexual or a homophobe which is a few steps on the other side of straight, you can benefit from learning this way of life in general. Just research it, talk to some of them and gain knowledge.

Online Only: Ok for whatever reason you choose this route, usually it is because you are already involved and just want the mental fun of it. If your other is aware of your online activities then by all means run wild.

But if you are online secretively you need to unplug your computer. Whether online or off, truth and honor count.

You need to fix what is going on in your life before you bring some unsuspecting person into the fold and fuck them up with your games. Be real whether online or off.

Kinkster: You're in it for the fun, the kink, and the various sexual adventures you can find. As long as you are honest with the people you deal with have fun, enjoy.

This life offers many different areas of kink and it alone is all some people need. We all have our kinks, some people just do kink and nothing else in the life and that is fine.

Being who you are is one of the biggest points I can't make enough.

Bimbo: This one is always interesting, if you wish to be some airheaded doll with big tits and modification to other parts of you I say go for it.

Being some man's arm candy bimbo isn't the worst that can happen to you. It is a way of life that I don't fully grasp but I accept it like any other type of life. If it brings you joy and freedom then that is all that matters.

These touch the surface on what is out there, if I did not list more it does not mean they do not hold importance. Any of them are important to the people who live it and I am in no way discounting that.

I just know to mention them all would be a huge project in just one manual. These give you an idea that many people have many different lives and each one has a mental dynamic to it that holds importance and clarity of mind.

No matter the life you choose be true to it as well as yourself and you can't go wrong in it. Value what you live and those who live the life they choose and accept that not everyone lives as you choose to.

That in no way means your choice lacks value, as long as you do so honorably.

Embrace the journey and ride out the storms, if you do this then you are richer in life than most people can ever hope to be.

Chapter Ten: Vanilla

This one has taken me awhile to think on, what I should say, how I should say it, what am I looking for by adding this to the manual.

All these questions and many more I have asked myself. In doing so I found the answer I sought. Like with anything I have to be true to myself and just let it flow.

What comes of it will, if I do it justice then great, if not well we all are on a learning curve in life and I am learning everyday like anyone else out there.

I sometimes feel like there is this silent war going on between the vanilla world and our world. It is as if the disgust and dislike is so thick you could choke on it.

I know I am not the only one to feel this and I know I am not the only one to step back and look at it from a new point of view that is not necessarily my normal view and outlook.

So much could be said against the vanilla world, the judgment they place on us, the everyday stigmas, the outrageous assumptions, the laws and the lack of acceptance for a world they cannot begin to comprehend and understand without being shaken into awareness.

They turn a blind eye for the things they don't understand or become rude, disgruntled and in some cases downright hostile. This is all true and then some, it is real and it is a sickness.

The reason I say sickness is anything that festers inside you with such judgment and dislike is not healthy and needs to be purged out of you, by you.

Not by myself, not by anyone in my world, but by you, yourself. No one can lead you to the truth of us, we can only open the door and hope you enter and understand us better.

We don't care if you continue to live you own life as you will, just learn to do it without judging those who choose not to live their lives the way you do.

On the flip side I have met many a vanilla who may not get this life I lead but they accept me for who I am, even if they think I am wild or a freak, that is ok, I am still accepted for it.

As a vanilla I think one of the biggest mistakes you can make is snap judging something you truly know nothing about. Knowledge is the key to wisdom, I urge you to learn who we are truly before you condemn us as sick, ill individuals.

That is no more who we are than if all of you are hookers on a corner selling yourself.

Whether you suffered abuse as a child, as an adult were beaten by another, raped or if you grew up in a strict household with religious overtones or a simple strict home that went with the guidelines of the vanilla society.

Whatever the case may be learn this and remember it, one man nor does one woman make the whole of a society no matter their place in it.

One person should not shape who you are or who you become, that choice is yours and yours alone to see to. To let one person without consent choose who you are to be and the rules you are to follow is letting them live your life, not you.

That is not living; it simply existing day to day in a box with no true color or light. To me that is true victimization of who you are and to allow it to continue by your own hand when you want to break free and be who you are is truly a shame.

It is not always easy to see the big picture; I get that and can understand it. There was a time I growled at everyone and disliked everyone, I blamed them all for what happened to me and for how I was.

I learned that is no way to live, that to do so is to dishonor who I am and that my friends is a way more unacceptable form of life than I was willing to allow myself.

Luckily I grew to see what was inside me and what was out there. It takes work, it is hard and scary.

Sometimes downright mind boggling but with perseverance the hardest thing can be learned with the right amount of time and effort.

There are some easy tools out there to help you better understand a life you have no clue about, a society of people you dislike or fear, or that you are so much like that you run from yourself.

Having a guide to learning is normal in anything you do and this society and life is no different.

We have the tools, the information and the help if you are willing to look for it and disregard all the circus bullshit you see out there or the sexual leanings.

I will be the first to tell you there are a lot of things kinky and perverted out there.

Some of them I am sure would horrify the shit out of you but the actual basis of this society and life choice has nothing to do with that.

As far as I'm concerned you are welcome to your *normal* sex even if you choose to study and grow under this life. Sex doesn't make you the person you are, it just happens to be bonus.

Like with each chapter in this book I am going to give you a list so you can better understand what you are dealing with and to shed some light on the fears you have.

So listen and learn what you need to know.

- **Judgment**
- **Prejudice**
- **Narrow Mindedness**
- **Fear**
- **Ridicule**
- **Loftiness**
- **Bigotry**
- **Escapism**

Judgment: If you come into this judging it you have lost half the battle in yourself. Forget what has been drilled into your head, what you think is correct; open your ideas and thought process to something new.

As if you have never heard about it and are simply curious to find out more. Judgment doesn't do anyone any good and often can make an ass out of you.

Prejudice: This is unacceptable no matter what life you lead or what society you are in. If you come here with that on your shoulders you will be shown the door. Neither skin color nor sexual orientation define a person, character does.

To be this way is not tolerated and I personally find it deplorable. If you need to down another for their life choices then you are not only a bully but a hypocrite. This is harsh maybe but damn true.

Narrow Mindedness: Snorts. The narrow minded person is the one who oftentimes sits alone in the corner, of curls up in bed by themselves. It is an empty existence and a cold one.

There is no joy in have a narrow mind, it weakens you and turns you bitter.

Fear: I can't say this enough, to live in fear of what others may say or think of you is such a waste of your life. You have so much value to add to this world and to be shut down is a shame.

Don't let anyone hold your head beneath the water so you cannot breathe or see, push back and come up for air and light.

Ridicule: You want to get on someone for the way they live, look to your own yard first, last I checked God was not walking upon this earth so until HE does learn your own house before you ridicule someone else for the way they run their home.

Loftiness: Darlin' we all put our clothes on the same way, you in no way are better than the person sitting next to you.

So put on airs all you like but the next time you look in the mirror look at your imperfections because just like the rest of us you have plenty of them too.

Bigotry: Just because I don't believe what you do, doesn't mean it is wrong and intolerance for those who don't believe as you do shows such a lack of intelligence and class.

All I can say is, you're in for one rude awakening when it comes time to step up and show your true self in the light.

Escapism: Look I get you want to escape your normal life and branch out into another life that seems risqué and downright decadent but truthfully you're just running from problems you need to face in your own life and self.

This life choice is not for you to hide in; it's for you to grow in. So first fix what is going on around you, and then come explore this society.

I do not want to get you to join my society, I am not here to *convert* you. I want to educate you, show you where you have been misled and to open your eyes.

What you do after that is your choice, your decision. Whether you learn to love this way of life or just go back to the vanilla way of life matters little to me as long as you have an insightful view when you do choose whichever life choice.

Until you have that knowledge and insight all you are doing is running on a hamster wheel spouting bullshit you know nothing about and there is no value in such words from you.

Live happy, live long but more importantly just LIVE.

In closing I have a few things to say. I remember years ago when I first got the idea I should write such a manual because I felt like M/s was not represented in literature like it should be.

That sooner or later someone would write it, well here I am years later writing it.

I am a blunt, tell it like it is kind of woman. I have no shame in who I am or what I do.

I live my life based on a set of values I truly believe in and yet I still keep my eyes open to learn another's point of view.

I have a low tolerance for a belief that is based on a fairy tale or outright lies but even so I try not to completely disregard that point of view.

I am not you and you are not me but I will help you, show you my life and teach you how I live. I would expect the same of anyone who lives any type of life.

Show me how you live, teach me your way and if nothing else you will have added to my knowledge and blessed me with even more insight into the world of people that I did not already possess.

I don't know it all and I don't pretend to, like you I am learning every day. Life is one big journey with many roads to choose from and many paths to walk on.

Whichever path and road you choose, as long as you made that choice with eyes wide open and a mind willing to see what is out there then you have chosen wisely for yourself and everyone your choice effects.

I have been in this life choice for twenty years no, a long time. I have made the mistakes, still make them.

I took roads I should never have even thought to journey down and I have wept down paths I have walked.

Life is never pure and perfect, each road, each path is a character builder to help you understand more clearly the roads and paths you must take in the future.

It may take you a few roads and path before you begin to get it right, but if you keep going and don't look back you will find the acceptance in yourself as well as the enlightenment you seek.

Thank you to all those who have enriched my life so much and brought joy and understanding to me.

Special thanks to several people: Ellis, without your friendship I do believe life would be a bit more dull. Your passion and acceptance of who you are is refreshing and humbling to see. Thank you my friend, I very much appreciate you.

To my daughters Sierra and Sage: Thank you for showing mommy just how imperfect she can be and for teaching me not to take life so seriously all the time, to let my hair down and laugh more.

To my parents: Thank you for not leaving me at the hospital when I was born. Yes, I am grinning. You have taught me more than anyone that I can be me without fear I will in some way be caste out. You taught me that no matter what I do even when you dislike it you still love me and accept me.

To my Husband and Dominant: You have taken this journey with me, through the ups and downs and crazy rides. You make me truly feel beautiful even when I think I look like the Grudge. Thank you for your love, support and understanding.

To those of my friends on Collarme in The Lounge: I have known some of you a long time, and there have been some outright insane moments. I have laughed and learned so much being around all of you that I am truly blessed knowing each and every one of you: Maralidris, NaamahsLove, Blooms, Annora, Wenwen, SDD, MM, Bliss, MsBadd, Roadwarrior, spankedbyVoodoo, Gloryus and so, so many others. Again thank you.

Thank you to those who read this, my it bring you a better understanding than you had before.

www.ingramcontent.com/pod-product-compliance
Lightning Source LLC
Chambersburg PA
CBHW060410290526
45791CB00002B/683